$\mathcal{P}$LAY $\mathcal{M}$E A $\mathcal{S}$TORY

A Child's Introduction to Classical Music
Through Stories and Poems

by JANE ROSENBERG

ALFRED A. KNOPF • NEW YORK

For my sweet little daughters, Ava and Eloise.
And for my big one, Melo.

ACKNOWLEDGMENTS
I wish to express my thanks to the following individuals: to Susan Dwyer, for suggesting I tackle a classical
music book for children; to the cellist Robert Martin and the pianist Svetlana Transky, for their invaluable advice;
to my editors, Janet Schulman and Sharon Lerner, for their desire to enrich children's lives with great music;
and to my husband, Robert Porter, whose insights into my work guided my hand throughout this book.

THIS IS A BORZOI BOOK PUBLISHED BY ALFRED A. KNOPF, INC.
Text and illustrations copyright © 1994 by Jane Rosenberg
Published in the United States of America by Alfred A. Knopf, Inc., New York, and simultaneously
in Canada by Random House of Canada Limited, Toronto.

Library of Congress Cataloging-in-Publication Data
Rosenberg, Jane. Play me a story / by Jane Rosenberg. p. cm.
Summary: A collection of poems suggesting images that might be evoked by pieces of classical music, from
"The Elephant" in "Carnival of the Animals" to "In the Hall of the Mountain King" in "Peer Gynt."
ISBN 0-679-84391-4 (book and cassette package)
1. Music—Juvenile poetry. 2. Children's poetry, American. [1. Music—Poetry. 2. American poetry.] I. Title.
PS3568.07855P57 1994 811'.54—dc20 93-33490
Book design by Mina Greenstein. Manufactured in the United States of America.
10 9 8 7 6 5 4 3 2 1

INTRODUCTION

CLASSICAL MUSIC IS A VIBRANT ART FORM that can excite and enrich young people. But beyond offering *Peter and the Wolf*, what can parents do to make this music come alive? We all know that children have open and eager minds and that if parents present the classical repertory with enthusiasm, chances are their sons and daughters will catch some of their joy. But what music should be presented, and how can it be made accessible?

My daughters, accustomed to watching opera on videotape while I worked on a book of opera stories, assumed that most pieces of classical music tell a story. Ava, the older one, upon listening to a symphony or concerto, would ask, "Mommy, what's the story of this music?" If the music had no narrative, I would talk about the instruments and the style of the piece. But if the music was programmatic (that is, suggested a story, mood, image, or event), an opportunity presented itself to involve the girls more deeply, and I would answer with a little tale. This led to all sorts of fun: drawing, dancing, play-acting, even creating Halloween costumes of the sultan's wife Scheherazade and the magic Firebird.

I'm not suggesting that everyone has the energy, focus, or time to devote to guiding their children through the vast classical canon. Nor am I assuming that all parents have a background in classical music. What I am suggesting is that a book and CD—with stories, art, and, of course, music—can introduce children of all ages to the delights of great music.

The ultimate goal of this book and CD package is to provide a starting point for an appreciation of classical music. The excerpts included will entertain young listeners while offering works of some of the major composers. The collection of music in this book is not meant to be definitive, since the repertory is so vast that any number of titles would be equally suitable. My hope is that these seventeen excerpts will excite your children so much that you will race to the local record store to buy the complete versions of their favorite selections. Once they are beguiled by these pieces, they will be receptive to other classical compositions. And it will be of little consequence whether a work is programmatic or not, because the music will speak to them with or without stories and pictures. In fact, the last selection on the CD, from Bach's *Brandenburg Concertos*, asks the reader to lay aside word and image and simply listen.

So push back the living room furniture and get ready to crawl on all fours like an elephant while Abigail and Abner bounce up and down like a kangaroo—or gnash your teeth like Baba Yaga the witch as Zoe and Zeke run away, squealing in delight.

PICTURES AT AN EXHIBITION

The Hut on Hen's Legs (Baba Yaga)

MODEST MUSSORGSKY

Drums pound, cymbals shudder.
Baba Yaga, the Bony-Legged,
leaps from her witch's hut on chicken legs,
jumps in her mortar,
spurs it on with her pestle,
and, hungry for dinner, sweeps across the sky.

Over fields, over forests,
Baba Yaga sniffs out naughty children.
With turnips and onions she simmers these souls
in a hearty Russian ragout:
gnashing, gnawing, munching, mashing
a banquet of bones and tea.

THREE GERMAN DANCES

"Sleigh-ride"

WOLFGANG AMADEUS MOZART

Call horn call
for the royal court ball
for crystal chatter in a sumptuous hall
as the snowdrifts climb
in triple fine time
and the sleigh speeds fast
over whitewashed grass.

Ring tinkle chime
how the winter winds whine
and the horses trot in a rhythmic line
while the ladies flush
and the gentlemen laugh
and the sleigh speeds on
to the king's repast.

THE NUTCRACKER

Dance of the Toy Flutes

PETER ILYICH TCHAIKOVSKY

Marzipan shepherdesses
with sweet tasty dresses
a candied delight
playing toy flute or pipe.

They plié to a joyful tune
(I'd like to eat them with my spoon)
almonds, sugar, whites of eggs
I think I'd start upon the legs.

THE FOUR SEASONS

Concerto in G Minor (Summer)
Summer Storm

ANTONIO VIVALDI

Shuddering
    rumbling
        violins thundering
Boreas, the North Wind,
blows a chill breeze
through Summer's golden hair.

Orchard
    meadow
        cornfield, vine
Bees swarm
sheep cower
as the storm rolls in.

Sunlight
    half-light
        heat and rain
Boreas, the Wind,
in a cloak of dark clouds
blackens the summer day.

Heat lightning
    sheet lightning
        thunderbolt, hail
Birds dart, sheep flee
as the swollen sky
choked with tears
floods the smiling countryside.

A Midsummer Night's Dream

March of the Elves

FELIX MENDELSSOHN

From his pillow in the acorn cup,
from his bed in forest wild
leaps the shrewd and knavish Puck,
Moonlight's wayward fairy child.

Pluck the strings and blow the horn,
a call to midnight revelry.
Fairy sprites will dance till morn
to the elfin melody.

Behold where song and sport collide
by rushy brook in meadow green.
Sister Moon pulls, like the tide,
sweet Titania, the fairy queen.

She darts from Oberon, her shadow king,
his retinue of bat and wren
who wish to curb her wandering
along the paths of mortal men.

But the queen and her fairy tribe,
Cobweb, Moth, and Mustardseed,
drink the dew with fireflies
and rush where sylphid footsteps lead.

CHILDREN'S CORNER SUITE

Cakewalk

CLAUDE DEBUSSY

When Chouchou leaves the nursery
the piano strikes a melody,
the cakewalk dance, the cakewalk prance,
all the rage from here to France.

The Ragdoll Boy, a toy most dear,
steps out and calls, "The coast is clear."
And on his arm he takes a girl
to lead her in the nightly whirl
of syncopated merriment,
of struts and kicks and compliments.

"Your dancing," coos one ragtime fan,
"tops that of Aunt Minervy Ann's,
the cakewalk belle from New Orleans,
whose fancy footwork I have seen.
Yes, you, dear boy, should 'take the cake,'
the pastry prize served on a plate."

"What care I for accolades,
my life's as sweet as lemonade.
I live to dance, my soul and me,
to spin cakewalking poetry."

Scheherazade

The Tale of the Kalender Prince

NICOLAI RIMSKY-KORSAKOV

A sultry violin weaves a magic spell,
beckons like the voice of Scheherazade . . .

Daughter of the King's Vizier,
she was as beautiful as the moon,
as wise as the stars,
a maiden of such eloquence
that to listen to her speak
was to hear the music of the spheres.

Having watched her father grow weary and sad,
one day she said, "Tell me your troubles."
"I fear for the lives of my daughters," he answered;
and, as she wished to know why, he continued:

"The Queen betrayed the King.
Her crimes were black as pitch,
her treachery pierced him like a knife.
No longer did he trust a woman's love
so off came the Queen's head.
Now, every night, I must bring a new bride
and each dawn he orders her execution.
My daughters may be next."

"Marry me to the King, Father.
I shall save the daughters of our people."
"Never," said the Grand Vizier,
"the sacrifice is too great."
But Scheherazade had the will of a tiger.
Try as he might, the Vizier could not change her mind.
"Have no fear," she told her father,
"I will teach the unhappy King to smile."

Scheherazade married the King.
To pass the bridal night, she asked,
"Sire, would you like to hear a few tales of marvel?"
The King looked curiously at his bride, who
smiled sweetly, betraying no trace of her plan.
Intrigued, her husband allowed her to begin.

She spun tales far into the night
and the bitter King was enthralled.
In the middle of one charming story
morning broke.
The clever girl fell silent.
His duties were pressing
but the King wished her to go on.
"What shall I do with her?" he pondered.
"By the Prophets, I will not kill her
until all this story is told!"

Dawn showered its golden light upon the palace
and still Scheherazade was alive.
The next evening she began again.

One tale followed another.
Her words unlocked the mysteries of exotic lands,
her poetry conjured the perfumes and music of the Orient,
her verses laid before him the beauty of the world.

Never did he weary of her tales.
Dawn broke each day
yet he postponed her death
to hear the end of one story
and the beginning of the next.
One night turned into ten,
ten into one hundred,
one hundred into one thousand.

Then, on the one thousand and first night,
Scheherazade said,
"My King, I have no more tales to tell;
I am ready to die."

"Scheherazade, you have calmed my heart
and filled it with love.
I have listened to your wise and smiling words
and now my soul is joyful."

And so, to the end of their days,
the King lived happily with his bride
and harmoniously with his subjects.
In his kingdom
children flourished and wisdom prevailed,
and the name of Scheherazade was praised forever.

Scenes from Childhood

Reveries

ROBERT SCHUMANN

Said Julius and Karl, on a warm afternoon:
Leave that gosh darn piano and silly old tune.
Though I loved that piano and sweet melody,
I loved my two brothers most desperately.
Sure I'll come play. So where shall we go?
To the banks of the lazy day river, you know.

To the banks of the Mulde, we scampered like mice.
The world was in spring, but the water was ice.
So we galloped and laughed over green meadows fair
and rode a cock-horse to the big market square,
to dear Papa's bookshop, and so we agreed
to sit ourselves down and have a long read.

The hour grew late and my eyes they did tire.
I longed for my bed and a nice cozy fire.
So I closed my book, kissed Papa good night,
and called for Mama to turn out the light.
She gathered me up like a pod with her pea.
Dear me, what a fine memory—
what a very remarkably fine memory!

Symphony No. 6 in F

"Pastoral"

Merry Gathering of the Country Folk

LUDWIG VAN BEETHOVEN

Squish
goes the mud through the toes of April
    Splash leaps
the frog in the guggling brook
      Buzz sigh the
bugs in the bower of greentime
        Toot pipes the flute
to the country folk.

Munch
mash the farmers as they feast on pheasant
    Chomp chew
the maidens as they dine on hare
      Crack snacks the
squirrel as he nibbles acorns
        Glug slugs the plowman
as he drinks his beer.

Stamping, whistling, farmhands fiddling
Dancing, twirling, dairymaids whirling
Gulping, thumping, frogs' legs jumping
All in a circle, all in a round,
swinging at the woodwinds' wild hoedown.

THE CARNIVAL OF THE ANIMALS

CAMILLE SAINT-SAËNS

The Elephant

Elephants sigh a lot.
Heavy-stepping, heavy-hearted,
perched on legs that can't get started.

Elephants sag too much.
Heavy-layered, heavy-lidded,
tailoring that's poorly fitted.

Elephants wheeze a bit.
Heavy-breathing, heavy-going,
an ungulate with two teeth showing.

Kangaroos

Kangaroos are a different story.
When bouncing,
they are in their glory.

Hungarian Dance No. 5

JOHANNES BRAHMS

Past the vines, through the bramble,
by a river decked with green,
on a warm and wind-swept night
hear the Gypsy jubilee.

In their tents and painted wagons,
round the campfire's crackling flames,
fortunetellers read the future
in the nomad caravan.

Etched in light, wolf-eyed beauties,
skirts unfurled in waves of red,
dance like muses on the mountain
to the Gypsy violins.

"Trout" Quintet for Piano and Strings in A

Theme and Variations I-III

FRANZ PETER SCHUBERT

I.

On a sunlight-spattered
insect-talking day,
a giddy trout
played tag with his tail
in a cold, clear stream.

On a whistle-on
wing-flapping day,
a keen violin
traced the trout
through the rushes and the reeds.

II.

On a sunlight-spattered
insect-talking day,
an old fisherman
cast a silken line
in the cold, clear stream.

On a whistle-on
wing-flapping day,
a lithe piano
accompanied the trout
across the limpid brook.

III.

On a sunlight-spattered
insect-talking day,
the merry trout
saw the hook
and blithely passed it by.

On a whistle-on
wing-flapping day,
a stout cello
tracked the trout
and urged him on his way.

PEER GYNT SUITE NO. 1

In the Hall of the Mountain King

EDVARD GRIEG

Peer Gynt hates to toil and slave,
    plow the land,
      seed the earth.
He'd rather dream of fortunes made
in far-off fairylands.

Roaming on a mountain top —
    idle days,
      wasted nights —
Peer Gynt wanders aimlessly
among the sighing trees.

He chances on a princess troll —
    dirty feet,
      pig-faced snout;
courts her with a wooing gift
of rags and dusty straw.

"Father is the Mountain King,
        palace grand,
        empire vast.
If you wed me right away,
his throne and gold are yours."

In haste they mount the wedding steed—
        stars ablaze,
        dead of night;
trot off to Rondë land
to meet the King of Trolls.

In the hall the trolls sing out—
        green eyes glint,
        thick lips smack:
"Cook Peer in a boiling broth
of oxen mead and brine!"

"Trolls and goblins, gnomes and dwarves,
        hear me now,
        I'm your King.
True, Peer has a human frame
but he's like one of us.

"Greedy passions, lazy ways
        suit my daughter
        to a tee,
and Gynt has enough of these
to match the meanest troll.

"We can pin a tail on him,
        bulge his eyes
        like a troll,
then he'll see the world askew
and black will look like white."

"You have not consulted me,"
        Peer replies
        angrily.
"I refuse to marry her;
the price is far too high.

"For your riches, land, and throne,
        I'd wed your
        ugly girl,
but no troll can scar my eyes
to alter what I see."

"Roast him! He insults her!"
        "Bite him! He deceives us!"
Young trolls whirling, old trolls screeching,
        coarse skin scaling, black blood boiling.

"Beat him! He defiles us!"
        "Kill him! He defames us!"
Old trolls swarming, young trolls pouncing,
        pounding, clawing, cracking, biting.

"Help me! Mother, Father!
        Save me! I implore you!"
Distant chiming, church bells tolling,
        trolls and goblins shriek and flee.
                Peer Gynt sighing, safe from torment,
                castles vanish, night reigns free.

Maple Leaf Rag

SCOTT JOPLIN

Piano rapping, heel rocking, firecracker keys,
stars collide as fingers fly across the ivories.

Music from the Maple Leaf fills the gaslit street,
wafts into the hot night air, sings beneath the trees.

Passersby hear the strains—intoxicating rag—
"The King is back to play for us his stoptimes and slow drags!"

Past the pushcarts, down the tracks, townsfolk run full speed.
Up the stairs, climbing fast, to the Maple Leaf.

"Joplin's here," they shout with joy, crowding in to see
the King of Ragtime, striking chords, a two-step harmony.

Jauntily he sits astride an old piano stool,
playing syncopations that were never taught in school.

Folks stream in, floor boards bounce, rafters shake away,
ties are loosened, hair's let down when Joplin comes to play.

$\mathscr{T}$HE $\mathscr{R}$ITE OF $\mathscr{S}$PRING

First Part: The Adoration of the Earth
The Augurs of Spring—
Dance of the Young Girls

IGOR STRAVINSKY

Yerk
      Drub, Drub, Drub.
Yerk
      Drub, Drub, Drub.

Yarilo the Sun, god of growing,
smile upon our Mother Earth,
feed the soil, bloom the Spring buds,
warm the stones, rear the trees.

Drub, Yerk
      Drub, Yerk.
Yerk
      Drub, Drub, Drub.

For you the young girls, faces painted,
from the river in a row
dance the Spring Dance, bow together,
praise the earth and roots below.

WATER MUSIC

Alla Hornpipe

GEORGE FRIDERIC HANDEL

King George of Germany ruled England
but the king was a lonely man.
"I need a friend," he said to himself,
"someone who understands me."
In walked George Handel, the German composer.
"I'm King of England," said the king,
"but I don't speak English,
so my subjects don't like me."

"Sire," said the composer,
"there is a language you can speak, known to all."
"What?" asked the king.
"Music," answered the composer.
"A royal celebration!" exclaimed the king.
"Compose the music! Prepare the barges!
We'll float up the Thames
and the English will understand at last."

Minuet, hornpipe, rigadoon, bourrée—
lords and ladies danced,
tailors and seamstresses twirled,
roses were strewn at the composer's feet.
Trumpets, flutes, horns, violins
rising in majesty, speaking to all,
honoring the king, the court,
the English people.

The river was calm,
the night balmy.
King George stepped on board,
England's nobility followed.
The royal composer bowed to the court,
the musicians bowed to the king.
The baton was raised,
the barges embarked.

Up and down the Thames
the Water Music echoed,
a sound so rich and noble
that all London raced to the riverbanks.
Shimmering on quiet waters,
light from a hundred torches danced,
but Handel's music burned brighter than flames
that fair summer night.

List of Selections

Johann Sebastian Bach   Ludwig van Beethoven   Johannes Brahms   Claude Debussy   Edvard Grieg   Geor

Frideric Handel   Scott Joplin   Felix Mendelssohn   Wolfgang Amadeus Mozart   Modest Mussorgsky   Nicolai Rims

Korsakov   Camille Saint-   Robert Schumann   Peter Schubert   Igor   Peter Ilyich Tchaiko

Antonio Vivaldi   van Beethoven   Joh   rahms   Claude Debussy   rd Grieg   George Frid

Handel   Scott Joplin   lssohn   Wolfgang Am   Mozart   Modest Musso   icolai Rimsky-Korsar

Camille Saint-Saëns   mann   Franz Peter Sch   Igor Stravinsky   Pet   chaikovsky   Johan

Sebastian Bach   Ludwig van   Beethoven   Johannes Brah   ude Debussy   Edvard Gr   George Frideric Han

Scott Joplin   Felix Mendels   Wolfgang Amadeus Mozart   Modest Mussorgsky   Nicolai Rimsky-Korsakov   Cami

Saint-Saëns   Robert Schumann   Igor Stravins   Peter Ilyich Tchaikov   Antonio Vivaldi   Johan   Sebast

Bach   Ludwig van Beethoven   Johannes Br   Claude Debussy   Edv   Grieg   George Frideric Han   Sc

Joplin   Felix Mendelssohn   Wolfgang A   Mozart   Modest Mussorg   Nicolai Rimsky-Korsakov   Camille Sa

Saëns   Robert Schumann   Franz Peter   ert   Igor Stravinsky   Antonio   di   Johann Sebastian   ch   Ludwig

Beethoven   Johannes Brahms   Claude Debussy   Edvard Grieg   George Frideric Handel   Scott Joplin   Felix Mendelss

Wolfgang Amadeus Moz   est Mussorgsky   Nicolai imsky-Korsakov   Camille   Saëns   Robert Schuma

Franz Peter Schubert   vinsky   Peter Ilyich Tch   Antonio Vivaldi   Johan   Bach   Ludwig v

Beethoven   Johannes B   Claude Debussy   Ed   George Frideric Hand   Scott Joplin   Feli

Mendelssohn   Wolfgan   ozart   Modest Mu   Nicolai Rimsky-Korsa   Camille Saint-Saëns

Robert Schumann   Fra   Schubert   Igor Stravinsk   Peter Ilyich Tchaikovsky   tonio Vivaldi   Johan

Sebastian Bach   Ludwig van Beethoven   Johannes Brahm   Claude Debussy   Edvard Grieg   George Frideric Ha

Scott Joplin   Felix Mendelssohn   Wolfgang Amadeus Mozart   Mod   Mussorgsky   Nicolai Rimsky-Korsakor

Camille Sai   aëns   Robert Schumann   Peter Schubert   Igor   travinsky   Peter Ilyich Tchaik   y   Ante

Vivaldi   J   Sebastian Bach   Lu   Beethoven   Johannes   ms   Claude Debussy   Edvar   Grieg   Ge

Frideric Handel   Scott Joplin   Felix Mendelssohn   Wolfgang Amadeus Mozart   Modest Mussorgsky   Nicolai Rims

Korsakov   Camille Saint-Saëns   Robert Schumann   Franz Peter Schubert   Igor Stravinsky   Peter Ilyich Tchaikovs

Antonio Vivaldi   Johann   stian Bach   Ludwig van B   hoven   Johannes Brahm   ude Debussy   Edvard Gr

George Frideric Handel   Joplin   Felix Mendelss   olfgang Amadeus Moza   st Mussorgsky   Nicola

Rimsky-Korsakov   Ca   aëns   Robert Schumann   Peter Schubert   Igor   vinsky   Peter Ilyic

Tchaikovsky   Antonio   Johann Sebastian Bach   dwig van Beethoven   Brahms   Claude

Debussy   Edvard Gri   ge Frideric Handel   Joplin   Felix Mendels   olfgang Amadeus Moz

Modest Mussorgsky   Nicolai   insky-Korsakov   Camille   äns   Robert Schumann   Peter Schubert

Stravinsky   Peter Ilyich Tchaikovsky   Antonio Vivaldi   Johann Sebastian Bach   Ludwig van Beethoven   Joha

Brahms   Claude Debussy   Edvard Grieg   George Frideric Handel   Scott Joplin   Felix Mendelssohn   Wolfga